D1257889

Contemporary
RACQUETBALL

Chuck Sheftel and Arthur Shay

cbi Contemporary Books, Inc.
Chicago

Library of Congress Cataloging in Publication Data

Sheftel, Chuck.
    Contemporary racquetball.

    Includes index.
    1.   Racquetball.   I.   Shay, Arthur, joint
author.   II.   Title.
GV1017.R3S53   1978   796.34   77-91179
ISBN 0-8092-7547-3
ISBN 0-8092-7584-8 pbk.

Published by Contemporary Books, Inc.
180 North Michigan Avenue, Chicago, Illinois 60601
Manufactured in the United States of America
Library of Congress Catalog Card Number: 77-91179
International Standard Book Number: 0-8092-7547-3 (cloth)
                                   0-8092-7584-8 (paper)

Published simultaneously in Canada by
Beaverbooks
953 Dillingham Road
Pickering, Ontario L1W 1Z7
Canada

Contents

1
Introduction

The game of racquetball is so new—less than ten years have passed since it emerged from paddleball—that the five or six thousand photographs I've made of the sport for the United States Racquetball Association (USRA) represent three-fourths of the association's archives. The contemporary books I've collaborated upon with racquetball's Babe Ruth—Charlie Brumfield; with its Mickey Mantle—young Marty Hogan; with Jean Sauser; Terry Fancher; and national director and editor Chuck Leve make up more than half of the hard and soft-covered literature available on the booming sport.

So why another beginner's book just now?

I asked the question of Robert W. Kendler, racquetball's original organizer and the president of the USRA. He replied, "Short of getting on that 20' x 20' x 40' court with a good instructor, the new player should have the advantage of a simple, commonsense guidebook—the more the merrier, because quality will ultimately sort out the good from the not so good, the useful from the overexplaining treatise."

Pro Jean Sauser, coauthor with me of *Inside Racquetball for Women* and *Teaching Your Child Racquetball* says, "Racquetball is so easy to learn—relative to tennis or golf, for example— that the sooner a player can develop good habits, the sooner he or she can move up the ladder into tournament play or simply become good enough to beat friends who have played longer but who did not have the guidance of a good book, or a teacher—or both."

Chuck Sheftel is the founder of the American Professional Racquetball Organization (APRO), national headquarters: 730 Pine Street, Deerfield, Illinois 60015, which he started as a means of getting fully qualified racquetball teachers into the more than one thousand new racquetball facilities. His organization is currently setting up a series of tests, seminars, and conventions to help professionals and would-be professionals teach the growing army of racquetballers.

I first met Chuck Sheftel when he was chief racquetball pro at the Court House clubs in Chicago. I photographed him as he instructed a group of racquetball-playing airline stewardesses. TWA's *Ambassador* magazine later said they had more requests for the racquetball-article issue than any other. I met Sheftel again when he was working as a tennis pro, his original occupation. The first question I asked him was how tennis was different from racquetball.

"I'm glad you asked that question," he said, "because more than half the recruits coming over to racquetball come from tennis." Following, in digest form, are some of the differences and similarities as perceived by Chuck Sheftel, now the general manager and chief racquetball and tennis pro at Forest Grove Swim and Racquet Club in Palatine, Illinois.

"First off, I believe that playing one of the sports will not in any way affect a player's performance in the other.

The precision of the deep shot to the base line or the angled volley in tennis, the drop shot, and the topspin are all part of the joy of tennis and worthy of a lifetime's devotion. The quicker demands of racquetball on the body, the more intense anticipation, faster decisions—not having to chase the darn ball—and the different muscle groups excercised are all part of the appeal of racquetball to players of both sexes.

"In common they both require mental dexterity, intelligence to devise good strategy, and the ability to handle more and more complex strategy as the player becomes more proficient. There's absolutely no question about the fact that it's much easier for a nonathlete to have fun with racquetball right away. In beginning tennis, you must spend a lot of time picking up or chasing balls. So if you're impatient to get going in a sport with terrific exercise potential that's not boring, then racquetball is it.

"In racquetball, after you learn the essentials, the basic strategy becomes hitting the ball to the front wall and forcing your opponent into an error or hoping he or she will make one, giving you a point or the serve. (In racquetball, you can only score when you have the serve.) So in racquetball you're always trying to 'kill the ball' while in tennis you're trying to 'put the ball away.'

"The major physical differences between the two sports are that in racquetball the wrist is a flexible cocking and uncocking conduit of the body's power to the ball. In tennis the wrist is generally firm. If one player plays both sports in the same season it is wise to remember Charlie Brumfield's simple description of the basic racquetball stroke: 'It's exactly like throwing a baseball, whether you are meeting the ball sideways or over your head. The wrist must snap as if you're throwing across the infield.'"

There are other differences, of course, and other similarities, but watching Sheftel teach several beginning classes in racquetball (about half of the students were also tennis players) gave me the notion of doing a book on what I regard as a rather unique teaching method: a minute-by-minute syllabus covering eight hour-long lessons. Ideally, the Sheftel method works best for two players beginning the sport at the same level, but there is also room for individual practice and drills for unequally matched players.

In actual practice, several thousand new racquetball players have taken the series of lessons that follow, with a 90 percent rate of success; that is, being able to control their forehands and backhands, serve well, and volley with an equal or better player long enough to get one of the glorious feelings in all sport, almost equal to winning—the feeling of having gotten a good workout while adding to your proficiency.

The fact that this proficiency is in the sport with the fastest growth rate, I believe, should add to the wonderful sensation that comes more quickly in racquetball than from any other sport I know.

2

Before entering the court

Equipment

Before entering the racquetball court, you should equip yourself with rubber-soled sneakers or tennis shoes (low cuts unless you have an ankle problem) that fit comfortably with sweat socks. If you know that jogging or running in short bursts gives you blisters, make sure your shoes are big enough to accommodate two pairs of socks. This cuts down on friction on the feet and, of course, potential blisters.

Shorts should be of a solid color, preferably white. White is the sportsperson's color in racquetball, because it gives your opponent the best possible background for seeing the ball.

Tee shirts of almost any variety are de rigueur for the male player; those with the most cotton absorb perspiration best. Tee shirts with bras underneath are preferred by women pros. Some manufacturers make blouses, and some men don't mind collars on their tee shirts. In play, most players wear their shirts over their pants.

Eye guards are recommended for beginners. Most pros don't wear them on the theory that other pros know exactly where the ball is at all times. Some lightweight ones are now on the market.

Various glove companies now make racquetball gloves. These prevent callouses from forming on the thumb. Some players cut about an inch off the fingers of these gloves, and two manufacturers, Champion and Saranac, make such gloves. Some players play bare-handed. Pros who play this way generally carry a small towel tucked into their shorts to keep the racquet handle dry. When that handle gets wet, the hand tends to slip, decreasing accuracy.

Choice of a ball is simple. Seamco makes the popular green 559 ball used on pro tours and also the 558 black ball, which is identical except for color. As the competition by racquetball manufacturers has increased to keep up with the growing numbers of players, other manufacturers have been trying to catch Seamco. AMF makes a good blue ball; Vittert and Wilson also make balls. There's even a ball that can be rejuvenated with a fierce-looking hypodermic needle, but it becomes slippery after a dozen games. A Chicago player who had the kit on his front seat while stopped for speeding to his racquetball game was reluctantly given a pass by a cop who thought he had nailed a drug addict. No matter which ball you use, soak it in hot water for about five minutes before you take it on court. A usable ball should bounce five feet when dropped from an extended arm. And don't throw away your old bounceless, worn-out racquetballs. They're great for kids to use while learning; turn them in at the desk. (One accountant I know deducts them.)

By far the most important decision the new player has to make when he or she is least equipped to do so is choosing a racquet.

Almost as much care and thought should go into choos-

A comfortable forehand stroke. Wrist is beginning to "break" properly. Opponent should be watching the hitter for a clue as to where the ball will go.

ing a racquet as into marriage, because some of the same factors are involved: compatibility, closeness, love, and the possibility of abandonment or worse if things don't work out.

Racquets come in many weights, handle thicknesses, and basic shapes. These shapes are the owl's head or roundish conformation, or some sort of teardrop variation. Charlie Brumfield, racquetball's greatest theoretician, believes that the circular head, though somewhat shorter than the teardrop, tends to reduce the twisting of the racquet in the hand at the moment of contact with the ball. Former true-blue tennis players generally find the transition to the tear-shaped racquet easier.

In general, most pros agree that there are great differences between the new generation of fiberglass racquets and the lightweight metal ones. The new player is not equipped to do much beyond trying out both kinds and, especially, the handles of thicknesses from 3 inches all the way to 4½ inches.

Pros believe that the relative flexibility of the two types of racquets in "feel" as they hit the ball is the determining factor in choosing one over the other. The fiber fills, which are having their day in tennis, are generally more flexible than metal. Brumfield used fiber for a long time, feeling that the fiber racquet helped enhance his (already magnificent) control.

Fiber racquets, he said, let you wait until the last split second to make a shot, sometimes permitting a somewhat softer swing. In a way-out theory, at which Brumfield has no master or even a peer, The Brum has told clinics of teachers: "The disadvantage of the flexible racquet lies in its very flexibility. Because of this flexibility, the hitting zone at the top of the racquet is inferior to that of a metal racquet; however, the edge response is not as good."

So what do you buy?

Go to the display counter of your local racquet seller and make your decision on fiber versus metal and on the handle, which is covered with rubber, leather, or some synthetic imitation. Grip the racquet as if you were shaking hands. If you have a small hand, the grip size should be around 4⅛ inches. As you wrap that hand around the handle, your middle finger should just about touch your palm at the heel of your hand. Take a few practice swings. Does it balance well? Simulate throwing a ball. Can you get a little wrist snap going, even before you take lesson one?

Racquetball's reigning woman for the past five years has been a wiry, wily Texan named Peggy Steding. Peggy has small, even delicate hands, but uses a 4⅝-inch grip. "How come?" I asked her at a tournament she had just won. "Simple, Art," she replied. "I'm an old tennis player and I don't get as much wrist into the ball as, say, a newer player just starting out. So I stick to a thick, tennis-sized grip."

But Steding is something special and something else; she continues to knock off challengers half her age. Charlie Brumfield feels the wrist is by far the most important part of the swing, so you'd be wiser to favor your wrist action in choosing a racquet.

Ideally, your club should have a box of racquets for you to try before you start taking lessons.

In recent months, young Marty Hogan has completely dominated the sport and, like a true champion, plays in a completely unorthodox manner. But he has introduced power to the game of racquetball, hitting hard and trying to kill just about every shot. He uses a fiber racquet made by Leach Industries, the San Diego company for which most of the pros work, and gets all the power he needs: 142 miles per hour on his serve alone the last time he was tested by radar!

On the other hand, Charlie Brumfield is currently hard at work restructuring his game from finesse and control to a power game thanks to the current somewhat faster ball (20 percent more bounce than three years ago) and the successful example of power-hitter Marty Hogan.

And what sort of racquet does Brumfield, the Master, use? Metal, that's what!

Of course, says racquetball's first pro millionaire, Leach Industry's Charlie Drake, "Marty Hogan and The Brum could beat most players alive using a Ping-Pong paddle!" Drake, by the way, achieved financial success not via prize money, though he did win a few thousand on tour, but by selling his share in Leach, which he helped develop into the racquetball industry's prime manufacturer, to Colgate Palmolive-Peet, which promptly hired Drake to continue presiding at Leach, turning out so many racquets of all kinds, shapes, and weights. This discussion is a guide rather than an endorsement.

You probably won't have much choice at first, but when you connect with a good pro shop or dealer and have chosen a racquet that has a good feel for you, if you're offered a choice of string tension, remember a few things.

Metal racquets play best at around thirty pounds of string tension. Fiber-filled racquets play best around twenty-six pounds, give or take a couple either way. The stiffer (higher) the tension on the strings, the faster the ball will zoom from the racquet. This may startle your opponent, but it gives you slightly less control than a lighter tensioned racquet, which tends to keep the ball on the strings a microsecond longer, just enough to "carry" the ball. If you have a tight racquet and don't have access to a restringer, keep the tight racquet at the bottom of your gym bag for a few weeks, until the moisture of sweaty gym clothes loosens the strings.

If you *still* haven't chosen a racquet or must choose between a leather and rubber grip, remember that the rubber grip offers durability. You can wash it every few weeks and it will feel like new. Rubber slips a little more than leather, but it wears longer. Leather just wears or molts away.

Gloves should be washed periodically and stretched out to dry on your hand, possibly while eating with your other hand.

The grip

The world's foremost authority on the racquetball grip, as he is on almost every other aspect of racquetball, is

Charlie Brumfield. For the beginning racquetballer who doesn't know who Brumfield is, I like to think of him as the sport's Babe Ruth on the one hand and Albert Einstein on the other.

Having worked on perhaps six hundred sports stories for *Life* magazine in its prime, for *Sports Illustrated,* and as ABC's Television still photographer at the 1976 Montreal Olympics, I can say that except for golf's Arnold Palmer and Jack Nicklaus, I have never worked with any athlete who could perform and analyze at such great levels as Brumfield. With the calculated risk of getting ahead of our lesson plan, here is Brumfield on the grip, adapted from *Winning Racquetball,* which I wrote with Chuck Leve:

"The one fundamental most beginning racquetball players have trouble with for the longest time is seemingly the simplest: how to hold the racquet. The wrong grip or even the wrong-sized grip can cost you 50 percent of your hitting power. To a group of a hundred advanced players and instructors at a seminar, Brumfield said, 'I can almost guarantee that no one at this seminar knows how to hold the racquet properly.' " The few snickers turned into frozen grins after Brumfield concluded the first half hour of his absolutely fascinating grip lecture.

1. The racquet head must be an extension of your hand; you can't manage this without a proper grip.

2. The objective of the grip is to hold the racquet in such a manner that when it enters the proper hitting zone, the racquet face is square (perpendicular) to the line of flight of the ball.

3. When hitting the ball, you want the racquet face pointed toward the proposed target—a spot on the side wall, front wall, or ceiling—not inclined downward, twisted sideways, or bent upward. You want square impact on the forehand and backhand.

4. Square impact makes it easier for you to aim the

Contemporary racquetball

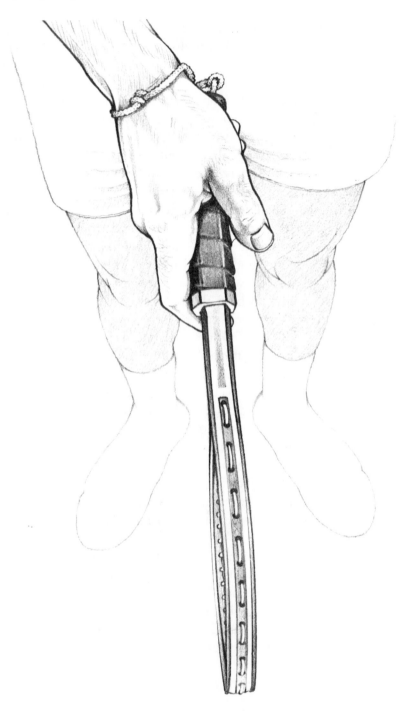

Forehand Grip

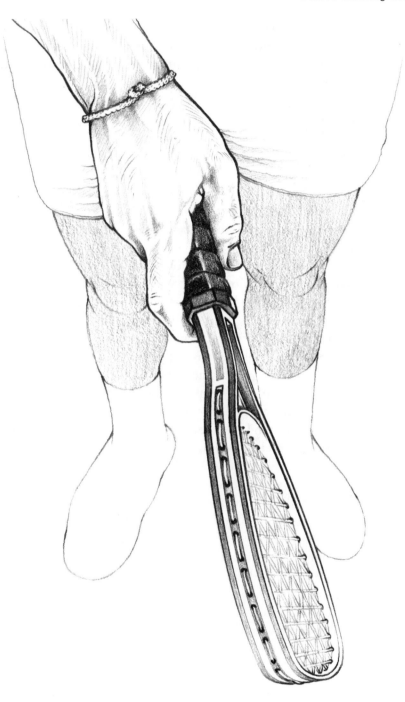

Backhand Grip

ball at your target. A square racquet face produces maximum power out of your swing, because any tilt cuts the percentage of power by the percentage of tilt. A mathematician, physicist, or computer can work this out; better, practice until you feel it yourself. As your swing becomes squarer to the ball, you will feel your power increase.

5. It will come as an early surprise to many new players that you can't get a square impact with the same grip on both sides, forehand and backhand.

6. For the forehand grip, hold the racquet handle as if you were shaking hands with it, with your hand midway down the grip and the face of the racquet up and down, parallel to the walls.

7. With this grip, you will notice that you have choked up slightly on the botton of the racquet. Brumfield's conclusion is that keeping the bottom finger about three-fourths to one inch from the bottom of the racquet gives the greatest flexibility to most players.

8. The emphasis on gripping the racquet should be on the last three fingers of the hand, unlike the tennis concept of finger spread or "fist grip." Also, don't pinch too hard with the thumb and forefinger—hang loose. If you apply too much pressure, you tend to freeze some of the arm muscles needed for a good wrist-cocking swing. You must not muscle the ball stiffly—swing your arm in a smooth arc.

9. A controversy exists on whether you should alter your grip slightly to meet a backhand shot (turn the face of the racquet floorwards) or change the entire arm motion to make the racquet meet the ball squarely. The easiest solution: let your racquet handle turn about a quarter inch as you chase a backhand shot. In a few months you may want to experiment with *not* changing your grip.

10. Racquetball is a sport like golf and baseball where a small person who can mass and release his or her power at

the moment of impact with the ball can hit with much greater power and accuracy than someone with big muscles and little coordination.

11. As the thumb and middle finger cradle the handle in a loose but controlling ring and the bottom two fingers provide a base for the grip, the forefinger (trigger finger in racquetball parlance) virtually lies along the upper shaft of the racquet, functioning similar to the stabilizing organ of a helicopter. "The feel of the grip should be in the fingers, not the palm," says The Brum. You're working for control, and control comes from the fingers, not the palm.

12. The final element in the racquetball grip is the "V" formed by the thumb and index finger around the handle of the racquet. Is the V too far over one way or the other as you look down your wrist to where your fingers grasp the handle of your weapon? Ideally, the point of the V should be right up the middle of the racquet, but you may want to experiment with the placement of that V after hitting a few shots.

13. You may hit the ball low, at thigh level, or at shoulder level, just as you might throw from any of those positions. The crucial thing to remember is that at the moment of impact the racquet face should be square to the ball.

If you have survived the gripping technical discussion above, you will easily survive all of the lessons that follow!

Using this book

Medical note

Racquetball can be a strenuous sport. Before getting started in racquetball, have your physician give you a complete examination, preferably including a stress test.

Warm-up

There frequently are a few minutes of waiting for the other players to vacate your court, "waiting for the bell," or just "early" time. In the locker room or hall outside your court, get into the habit of "warming up" for your hour of racquetball. Ten knee bends, a hundred slow jogs in place, and about two to three minutes of body stretching or pushing against a wall are gentle ways to prepare your body for racquetball. Jogging in place is especially good as a single exercise, as is holding your racquet by the handle and extending it down your back until you grasp the head with your other hand. Let your hands seesaw the racquet to stretch your arms.

Do these warm-ups before each of the lessons.

One more thing: start your lessons with at least one can of good balls—they're packed in twos. But also ask your friendly court club manager to let you use about six to ten older balls. This will save beginners lots of walking-around time.

This book represents the first appearance in print of a series of eight lessons that several thousand persons have successfully taken. As noted earlier, the lessons are designed for two beginners who can work with each other.

Each lesson takes an hour to complete properly and is so designed that slower students can repeat them until they feel they've got the lesson right. Similarly, players who can only play once a week may want to repeat several of the lessons en route to proficiency. So set your own pace.

At the beginning of each chapter-lesson will appear an outline of what should be accomplished in the hour. Moreover, the time allotted for each section of the lesson is given in minutes, and the time is again suggested at the start of each lesson. ("Suggested" because some areas of play may come more quickly than others to certain players.)

3

First lesson

1. Discussion of basic rules of play   (5 minutes)
2. Basics of the grip: forehand and backhand   (10 minutes)
3. Drills
    a. Side-wall drill   (5 minutes)
    b. Partner feeds to hitter on forehand side   (15 minutes)
    c. Partner feeds to hitter on backhand side   (15 minutes)
4. Play   (7 minutes)
5. Wrap-up   (3 minutes)

Discussion of basic rules of play

A good, shorthand summary of racquetball rules has been written by pro Jean Sauser, the nation's fifth ranked women's pro, who plays for Leach Industries and instructs at Sky Harbor Club in Northbrook, Illinois. This is Sauser's summary, from her book *Inside Racquetball for Women.*

1. A racquetball game is played to 21 points. You have to be only one point ahead to win the game. Winning two

To practice lob serve, ball is dropped from high, with racquet held low.

Racquet moves under ball to lob it high to wall.

out of three games gives you the match. The tie-breaking game may be 11 points.

2. Only the server can make points.

3. If the receiver wins a volley, the receiver wins the serve.

4. The object of racquetball is to win volleys and thereby make points.

Serving

1. The server must stand in the service zone, bounce the ball, and hit to the *front wall first*. After hitting the front wall,

Lob serve is made, high on wall, usually aimed to opponent's backhand, deep in court.

the ball may or may not hit one side wall and then bounce past the short line into deep court.

2. You get two attempts to serve the ball correctly. The following serves are faults, any two of which in succession result in a side-out (loss of serve).

a. Short serve: The ball fails to clear the short line. (Touching the line is a short serve.)

b. Long serve: The ball goes to the back wall on the fly.

c. Three-wall serve: The ball hits two side walls before bouncing in deep court.

d. Ceiling serve: The ball hits the ceiling on the way to deep court.

23

3. You will lose your serve on your first attempt if:

a. You fail to hit the front wall first.

b. The ball hits you on a bounce or a fly as it comes off a wall.

Receiving

1. The receiver stands in deep court, midway between the forehand and the backhand side walls.

2. The receiver may hit the ball on a bounce or fly. The ball must then return to the front wall without touching the floor. Any combination of walls the ball hits on its way to the front wall is legal as long as the front wall is included in every volley.

Volleying

1. Once the ball bounces on the floor twice it is out of play.

2. If the ball touches your opponent on the way back to the front wall, a "hinder" (for "hindrance") is called and the point is replayed.

3. If your opponent is hit by a ball coming off the walls on a bounce or fly, he or she loses the volley.

4. If you are hit by your own shot coming off the walls on a bounce or fly, you lose the volley.

5. If your opponent makes an attempt to move out of the way to allow you a clear shot at the ball but is unable to do so, a "hinder" is called and the point is replayed.

6. If your opponent deliberately does not move to allow you a clear shot at the ball, an "avoidable hinder" is called and she or he loses the volley.

7. A "screen ball" is called when your opponent blocks your view of the ball. The point is replayed. Most "screens" occur on serves.

Basics of the grip: forehand and backhand

Applying what you've learned in the prelesson discus-

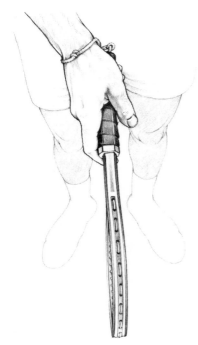

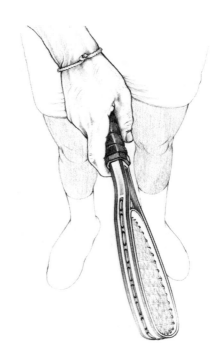

Forehand Grip   Backhand Grip

sion of the grip, you should now grasp the racquet as if shaking hands with it. Some beginners find it helpful to use their off hand to help the face of the racquet assume its position parallel to the side walls. Keep the V in mind—the V formed by your thumb and forefinger as they encircle the handle of the racquet.

The Sheftel method strongly advises the beginner to start immediately on altering the forehand grip for a backhand shot by moving the fingers ever so slightly, giving the racquet an eighth of a turn, between a quarter and half an inch in a downward direction. This makes up for the different distance and angle the racquet hand traverses when hitting a backhand shot. At the moment of impact with the ball, of course, both strokes call for the racquet face to be straight up and down to assure a smooth powerful stroke that accurately sends the ball to the front wall.

Drills

Side-wall drill

The student faces the side wall while standing in the dead center of the court. The object of this simple beginning

drill is to bounce the ball and *gently* hit it straight ahead to the side wall. The object is to get the feel of tapping the ball and of the power locked up in those strings. A rudimentary feeling for accuracy—making the ball return to your basic position—can be gained during this drill. It may feel like child's play, but getting the feel of the racquet on the ball is a basic step in learning the game, so don't take this drill lightly. It's also fun.

This drill should finish with a few backhand "pats" to the same side wall, again, just for feel.

Partner feeds to hitter on forehand side

Alternating during this time period, one student should now take up a position well back in the center of the deep court, about four feet in from the rear wall.

The other student (or more advanced player, if the players are unequal) should stand in the left side of the serving area and attempt to hit the ball to the wall and have it carom to the other player's forehand side. This player should attempt to hit the ball back to the front wall.

A partner without sufficient control to do this at this

stage could use his or her racquet arm to *throw* the ball at the front wall, remembering to try to snap the wrist at the moment of release (this is the basic racquetball wrist snap).

Players should alternate until the first fifteen minutes are up.

Partner feeds to hitter on backhand side

Same as the previous drills, alternating for fifteen minutes. Both players should begin to get a sense of the game by the end of these exercises, to the extent that they may break out into a healthy rash of volleying lasting three or four shots.

If a better player of sympathetic nature appears on the balcony, if your court has a balcony as many do, you might prevail on him or her or your friendly local pro to hit balls to your forehand and backhand in random sequence, so you get used to loping across the court to take your shots and do not become mired in one area.

The keys to racquetball are mobility and power. After you achieve mobility, your body will gradually provide more and more power. Running to meet the ball and hitting it smoothly is the basic achievement that must be accomplished by the new player.

If for any reason you find yourself on the court all alone at this stage, use the time to "feed" yourself. Try to hit the ball off the front wall to your forehand. Do this for a few minutes until you feel that you have a certain amount of control and can predict where the ball will land as it comes back from the wall. Don't make this exercise too easy if you seem good at it. Run a few steps to meet the ball—to the right if you're right-handed and practicing your forehand, and to the left to practice your backhand. (The 15 percent of us who are left-handed know how to reverse all these directions or should practice in front of a mirror until they can make the basics fit.)

The point is that pros spend a great deal of time—up to five or six hours a day—practicing specific shots and aspects of their game and use their solo time on the court for repetitive drills on shots they are perfecting.

In your few minutes of solo time, don't hit aimlessly. Have a goal: left side, right side, running to get the ball, hitting it back to your weaker or stronger hand. Brumfield has been known to practice his backhand "pinch" shot—a shot that goes down the left wall, hits the left wall a couple of feet from the corner, then caroms off the front—some five hundred times at a session! Ten or twenty shouldn't be too much for you.

Play

OK, play racquetball, even if you feel like a turkey at it! Start with a good legal serve, trying not to hit yourself with the ball coming off the wall, and return your opponent's return, if it's legal!

Serves should be alternated in practice. Here server serves to forehand of partner. This drill can be expanded to include "touch and go." Receiver must touch wall with racquet, then get back to the shot.

30

Wrap-up

A short self-coaching session: take a few minutes to recap the drills you've done and the shots you feel you need work on.

4

Second lesson

1. Warm up before entering court (jogging in place, knee
   bends, stretching, etc.)   (5 minutes)
2. Review briefly the grip and the basic forehand and
   backhand strokes   (2 minutes)
3. Your stance: Assuming a ready position   (2 minutes)
4. Refining the basic strokes   (8 minutes)
5. Studying off-the-back-wall shots and angles   (8 minutes)
6. Alternate with your partner at lobbing shots to the back
   wall and returning them to the front wall (11 minutes)
7. Play   (16 minutes)
8. Wrap-up   (3 minutes)

Warm-up

Warm up before entering court (or on the court if the
court is empty before your hour begins).

Review the grip and forehand and backhand strokes

Remember that it is the fingers that accomplish the slight turn of the racquet for the backhand grip, and that this turn occurs as you race to meet the ball on your backhand side. Keep looking down at where your thumb and forefinger make that all-important V on the racquet handle. Hit a few shots to the wall, aiming waist high for accuracy, with the V dead center on the handle, then vary the V slightly, first to the right then to the left. Note the effect this slight shift has on the direction of the ball. Resolve to keep that V straight up, except for a backhand shot.

After a few months of play, you may want to experiment with the placement of this V and with not shifting your grip that quarter-inch for the backhand. But for now, be a good, average student and try to become an orthodox player with a dependable, improvable style—the kind of player for whom this lesson plan was designed and has worked extremely well.

Your stance

Racquetball is primarily a sideways game. You generally hit the ball while facing one side wall or the other.

However, your ready stance should keep you alertly facing the front wall. To receive the ball (receiving the serve will be covered in the next lesson), go into a slight crouch, balanced on the balls of your feet. Be ready to move in any direction, turn your body sideways on the run—facing the right wall for a forehand, the left wall for a backhand—and hit the ball in a smooth arcing swing.

To begin, position yourself in center court about a racquet's length from the rear wall. Crouch forward alertly, with the body's balance forward. The ready position is the same as in tennis, which you know from your own tennis career or from watching the pros on television. Alertness and readiness to chase the ball are the keys, with one slight

difference. In racquetball, it's a good idea to carry the racquet slightly higher, with the top of the racquet pointing to the ceiling and its face parallel to the front wall.

The reason for this is simple. As noted, the cocking and uncocking of the wrist, like in a snap throw, is vital to transmitting the body's power down through the arm to the racquet and the ball. Carrying the racquet aloft helps you snap that wrist with a slight turnover motion when you actually hit the ball. This is more easily felt than explained, and you will feel it more and more as you practice. When you feel the wrist snapping properly that first time, you'll remember it and work to achieve the feeling in subsequent shots, both backhand and forehand.

Marty Hogan's unorthodox superhigh racquet position has been called a "coiled spring" by Charlie Brumfield. As Hogan hits, the racquet uncoils a tremendous amount of body, arm, and wrist power at impact with the ball. You won't be able to hit faster than 140 miles per hour at the beginning, but it's something to think about if you're fairly strong and your shots are just barely reaching the wall, despite a powerful swing. The crucial component is the wrist snap, which delivers the power from the body to the ball.

And the entire transmission system begins with the stance!

The forehand

Imagine the racquetball stroke as a crescent that starts well back and high, meets the ball at the center of the crescent, then follows through by rising to the other side of the crescent. A controversy currently rages among pros about the point on the crescent at which the ball is met.

Marty Hogan "is so powerful a hitter," says Brumfield, "that he creates his own shots and hits anywhere along the crescent he finds himself, muscling the ball to the wall by sheer strength and accuracy. He hits two or three feet back of where most players hit."

The orthodox method—hitting the ball off the front foot—is probably much safer for you. Practice getting your body into position so that the crescent of your swing is at midpoint as the ball comes in line with your front foot. The process of getting the body into the swing is very much like the baseball player at home plate. He or she waits for the pitch, weight balanced and slightly forward. As the swing begins, the weight goes momentarily to the back foot, then thrusts forward so that the body's power is transmitted to the ball at the moment of impact. Golfers too will feel at home trying to develop a powerful, accurate, coordinated swing in racquetball. Just imagine the trough of that crescent around the area of your front foot—low, medium, or high doesn't alter the "where" of that crescent. You will just have to start your crescent a little higher or lower (overhand shots will be discussed later).

The backhand

In a group of racquetball students, those who develop a

Refining the basic strokes

good backhand will generally make the fastest progress. What must be avoided is "taking everything with the fore-hand," even if it's a good forehand. This one sidedness is a bad habit that generally develops early in a racquetball player's career, and usually doesn't make much difference until he or she runs up against a better player. This player will then proceed to crowd the opponent to one side of the court or the other, then pepper the far side with shots the person with no backhand can't possibly reach because he or she has left fully half the court unguarded.

Backhand shots for accuracy should be attempted in this drill. Aim down the left wall, trying to catch it just short of the corner. It is especially important in practicing the back-hand to keep that front foot aimed at where you want the ball to go.

The overhand

The stroke that seems to come most naturally to rac-quetball players is the overhand stroke. This is a natural overhand baseball throw type of swing—a pitcher's motion with a racquet attached. It has had relatively few uses in racquetball, but recently it has begun appearing in the arse-nal of certain pros as a power stroke, not unlike the tennis serve.

The trick to the overhand is not letting your elbow lead your arm into the shot. This results in a great loss of power and ultimately to elbow trouble. Racquetball players with no baseball or softball-throwing experience should grab for an imaginary ball behind their right ear and attempt to throw it out straight from that position. This exercise will keep the elbow well back. Now all you have to do is add the racquet. The overhand is used against balls that come at you above shoulder level. (Do not confuse the overhand stroke with the "ceiling ball," an advanced maneuver discussed in the final chapter of this book.)

Overhands are most effective when they propel the ball low into the corners, but many a point is lost because of the tendency to hit the floor first unless you practice them.

Studying off-the-back-wall shots and angles

In most sports, the ball generally comes at you from the front as it often does, of course, in racquetball. However, many racquetball shots come at the player off the back wall. This opens up an entirely new area of judgment. The purpose of this lesson and drill is to teach this judgment.

Remember, when playing a ball off the front wall your body must move from side to side. When the ball hits the back wall, you must adjust to moving up and back. (Of course there is some lateral movement, but we're talking about the principal adjustments in thinking and body position.)

A crucial judgment for the beginner to back-wall play is gauging where the ball will bounce after it hits the back wall. The closer the ball bounces to the back wall before hitting it, the further out it rebounds. The further from the back wall it bounces en route to hitting it, the closer the ball rebounds, generally speaking.

At this point another difficult judgment area arises: the ball comes towards the back wall at any angle, hits the floor near the back corner, then angles out sharply.

Students should become aware at this point that a ball that angles into the right corner will come out to the left and vice versa, whether hitting the front or the rear corners of the court. It is in learning to play these angled shots that the well-coordinated player with natural alertness or what the TV commentators call "quickness" will do well. It takes many practice shots for most beginners to become adept at figuring angles and to solve the difficult problems of "hitting off the back wall."

The first rule is never rush the ball—wait for it to come to you. Racquetball appears to be a lightning-fast series of

(Upper left) For most beginners the racquet should contact the ball when the ball is off the front or lead foot. Ideally this foot should be pointing towards the front wall, or wherever the player wants the ball to go. In this illustration the player is striking the ball off the rear foot and his front foot is pointing away from the front wall. There errors will result in a loss of power and a loss of direction. As a player improves he or she may want to experiment with hitting the ball further back in the stance—that is, off the rear foot—but this doesn't work well for most players (only for the most powerful). In general racquetball is a sideways game with most shots made facing one side wall or the other. The "open" stance illustrated here most often occurs in a panic situation such as racing to make a shot coming off the back or side wall before you're ready to meet it with a proper stance. *(Upper right)* This is a much improved body position for meeting the ball—if contact is made as the ball flies past the front foot. *(Bottom)* This is a good follow through, with racquet ending up pointing to the front wall. The racquet can swing even higher to complete its arc. The important thing is a rhythmic, not choppy, stroke.

movements, but broken down into its components it is largely a waiting game. There is often more time than you think. There will be mad rushes too, of course, but we are speaking about the majority of shots. There is almost always time to get into a good receiving stance; racquet up, wrist ready to cock, front foot facing your target on the wall.

There is a tendency for beginners to overrun the ball on corner shots that go in and come out about waist high. Here the waiting game is crucial.

Almost every beginner seems to rush the ball. As you develop your game you will be able to save your rushes for when they really count—those low shots up front and ones that have passed you on one side or the other, for instance.

Bearing in mind whatever you can retain, alternate with your partner at lobbing shots to the back wall and hitting them back to the front wall. Try to compute the angles the

back-wall balls will make as they come out of the rear corners and get into your ready position in time to meet the ball properly. Aim some low, medium, and high shots at the corners just for the fun of it and also to judge where the ball will go—then run to the right spot at the right time.

Lob some of these practice shots into the back wall on the fly, so that they may legally bounce once on the floor before you hit them. This is a little easier to master at this stage than shots that bounce on the floor close to the rear wall and scoot out fast, which must be taken on the fly.

Play

You should now challenge each other with practice shots and volleys based on this lesson: forehands, backhands, and those frustrating back-wall shots, angles and all. Don't

rush the ball if it comes at good, playable height. The important things are getting set, facing those side walls as you swing, and *always* carrying that racquet high, wrist cocked and ready to snap during your stroke. A good time to practice your waiting game is when playing balls coming down from the ceiling or from high on the side walls. There's usually enough time to turn your body sideways, forehand or backhand, and take a good swing rather than a stab.

Wrap-up

Practice what you think are your weakest areas or at

Much improved stroke. The pupil has begun the stroke with her feet pointing to the side wall and with her knees slightly bent. Her body pivots comfortably at the right distance from the ball, and her shot probably is just fine.

least discuss them with your partner. Go down the list of what you've practiced during this hour. If you're not too tired and there are other empty courts, and the management doesn't object (as it generally doesn't), continue with some creative free play, incorporating what you've learned where possible. If both of you need back-wall practice, work with each other on this.

The difference between flailing around at the back wall and taking shots off it with respectable accuracy is often a matter of two hours of cumulative practice. Once you learn to judge this crucial racquetball shot, you will be able to refine it from a good defensive tool into a powerful offensive weapon. But goodness, this was just your second lesson!

5

Third lesson

1. Warm up before entering court   (5 minutes)
2. Review briefly the technique of taking shots off the back wall (take a few angle shots for a refresher)   (5 minutes)
3. Explanation and practice of the lob and drive serves   (10 minutes)
4. Short discussion of doubles and cutthroat and positioning for doubles and cutthroat   (6 minutes)
5. Drills
   a. Lobbing on the serve and for back-wall shots   (8 minutes)
   b. Serve the drive   (8 minutes)
   c. Point and serve, with return   (10 minutes)
6. Play   (10 minutes)
7. Wrap-up   (3 minutes)

Warm-up

Warm up before entering court if possible. Jog in place,

47

Good eye and racquet coordination is shown in this excellent stroke. The ball is hit well out in front of the body. This is what the good student's swing should resemble.

The feet are, of course, an important part of the racquetball stroke. Here the student's feet have become criss-crossed and her chances of stroking the ball properly are diminished because the body resembles a pretzel rather than the coiling and uncoiling spring it should be for racquetball.

do stretches and the racquet-down-the-back stretch with left hand tugging the racquet away from the right hand. Add ten sit-ups.

Review

Alternate with your partner at hitting or throwing the ball to the rear wall at various angles, then hitting the ball to the front wall. After each of you has successfully accomplished this, try hitting the same shot to the left corner and then the right corner of the front court, waist high or lower. If you prove proficient at this, add a little power with your cocked wrist.

The lob serve and the drive serve

The lob serve is deceptively simple. The player just stands in the service zone and hits a relatively easy shot.

Lob serve is made, high on wall, usually aimed to opponent's backhand, deep in court.

Characteristically, this shot hits high off the front wall, then bounces back a few feet past the short line near the left wall, right to the opponent's backhand. The opponent generally will have to move towards the wall to make a return and often he or she will try to clobber the slow-moving ball and bobble it in the attempt.

To serve this ball to the left, start serving a little to the right of center. To make it go right, stand a little left of center.

Most pros use the lob as a second serve after missing with an ace—an unreturnable serve—on the first serve.

A good lob should not go too deep into the court because it could easily bounce, hit the back wall, and come up for an easy kill shot by your opponent.

At this stage of your development, you should use the lob as a good sure way of getting the ball across the short line to your opponent. The more of a power hitter your opponent is, the more frustrating to him or her will a nice puny lob be.

As you advance, you will learn to use the lob as a nice change of pace after you notice a certain tenseness or tightness in your opponent, who was expecting you to powder the ball.

The drive serve is a low forehand, hit solidly on a line to the wall. The body's weight should shift from the rear foot to the front foot as you swing about knee high. Generally, it is aimed about three or four feet from the corner on the left front side, and it comes back to your opponent's forehand a foot or two past the short line, ideally going dead as it hits the point at which the floor joins the wall, for an ace.

Doubles and cutthroat

Mixed doubles and "cutthroat" are growing in popularity. For one thing, three or four players on a court cuts down the cost of play. More importantly, doubles play is fun.

Player prepares to turn around for a quick glance at opponent's handling of his serve. This should be an over-the-left-shoulder look.

The basic thing to practice and remember in doubles is that each player should play one half of the court as if that half were his or her own entire court. Shots at or near the center should generally be taken by the player with the closest forehand. In case of potential collision, players should resort to one or the other using "the only two words that should be spoken on the court," according to USRA President Bob Kendler, which have been widely accepted since he introduced them into handball: "mine" and "yours." The first player to say either word designates the taker of the shot.

In summary, doubles play at your stage of development gives you a court that's only 10 feet wide but 40 feet long. Wear safety glasses in doubles because you can be easily hit by a racquet.

In "cutthroat," where three continuous scores are kept—the server against the other two players—the trick is to use your numerical advantage to keep the single opponent off balance and racing from side to side and front to back.

Cutthroat is also excellent exercise for a good player opposing two beginners, especially one who likes to run a lot.

Drills

Lobbing for back-wall shots

This is a practice regimen in which novice partners can be of great help to each other. The idea is for the server to practice lobbing the ball to the receiver in different areas of the deep court. Hitting these lobs a little higher and a little

Instead of waiting for the ball to come just a bit more forward, towards her front foot, she has rushed her swing, bobbling the ball and causing her instructor to scratch his beard in dismay.

deeper will cause them to hit the floor in deep court and bounce to the back wall. The receiver must then return the shot off the back wall.

These lobs can be angled into the deep corners, giving the receiver practice at playing those angles. Alternating gives both players this kind of crucial practice. Think of the lob serve as an extremely basic tool, especially if your accuracy is slow in developing. The lob is a good safe shot that the pros almost always use as a second serve and as a change-of-pace tactic against a tense player.

If three or four of you have remained on the court after doubles or cutthroat, practice lobbing to alternate sides. All players can in this way get some practice, either serving or returning. Let these serves and returns blossom into volleys. Keep them going if you can.

The drive serve

After two, three, or all four players have achieved a degree of accuracy at the lob serve and return, you are ready for the drive.

The drive is more difficult than the lob because it is a faster, more powerful shot requiring somewhat more accuracy in its execution. You must keep your body weight well back until you swing and meet the ball with the racquet straight up and down, aimed at the front wall. Your body should be parallel to the side wall, with the front foot pointing to your target on the front wall.

After you hit the drive serve, you must take a swift peek at your opponent and step back a couple of feet from the short line to take up a center-court position, which will be discussed in the Fifth Lesson. For now, you should understand that when you serve hard and fast you're likely to get a return shot that's equally hard and fast. Be ready for it, because you will have somewhat less time to set up your defense when play begins with a drive than with a lob.

Perfect server and receiver positions. Note receiver is bent slightly forward, alertly ready to go wherever the ball is. Server will, ideally, turn around in the instant after serve, to see his opponent's shot and thus gain a jump on his next shot.

Point and serve, with return

At this stage of your racquetball progress, you should be able to predict where on the front wall and, by extension, where on the court your serves will go.

This is where you get a chance to do the Babe Ruth number—point to a spot on the court and hit to it. Do series of three serves to one spot in the receiver's court. Let your

In the point and serve drill, the server predicts where his serve will go, giving his partner time to get set properly.

receiver (or receivers if you're now practicing with two or three other players) return your predicted serves as well as he or she can. Keep the volleys going.

Ultimately, of course, you will try to mask your serves' intentions, incorporating a degree of deception and surprise in your game. (Brumfield says that Hogan could make five more points a game if he would make his 140 miles per hour serve more deceptive!) But long before you are ready to deceive your opponent, you must develop enough control to put the ball where you want it to go. This, as in all other ball sports, is called "control."

Play

Whether you are working out with one, two, or three players in this lesson, you should use this ten-minute free-play period to work on your weaknesses and, if it's a friendly, constructive group, on everyone elses. If someone needs more drive-serve practice, let him or her have the time. As receiver, work on positioning yourself for the shot and getting sideways so that you can get the power inherent in your body behind the ball. This gradual growth of confidence begins in racquetball after you've made a few good zinging shots. The swing feels good and the racquet meets the ball off that front foot or a little behind it, if by experiment you find that's where the crescent of your swing imparts the most power.

The point is to practice creatively with goals, rather than just hitting the ball around at random.

Wrap-up

More of the same. Take a one-minute break and see if you can find agreement with your partner or partners on what each of you has been doing both right and wrong. Errors that baffle you are sometimes easily visible to others. Two common correctible faults at this stage: not bending from the trunk enough to meet the ball and "scooping" at the ball underhanded like a softball pitcher, instead of getting sideways.

6
Fourth lesson

1. Briefly review the serves and returns   (2 minutes)
2. Explanation of center-court positioning   (8 minutes)
3. Drills
   a. Serve and return practice   (10 minutes)
   b. Touch and go   (10 minutes)
   c. Around the world   (10 minutes)
4. Play   (17 minutes)

Warm up before you get on the court, as usual. Now you might want to add a couple of minutes to your regimen. More sit-ups are good for the waist and also to get the blood pumping. If your court is available early, start hitting a few slow shots, preparing your eyes and body for the learning hour. Do knee bends to loosen the long leg muscles. You're getting to be a racquetball player!

Reviewing the serves and returns

Start with the lob and after a few series of lobs and

Receiving a serve to the backhand side, the woman has stepped off with the wrong (left) foot first. This will get her to the ball with her body facing the front wall not the side wall. Remember, racquetball is a sideways game. Hitting the ball from an "open" (facing front wall) position results in loss of almost all of the body's power except a portion of arm power.

Watching opponent, player gets an instant feeling for where he must be for his next shot. Note woman's feet are facing side wall properly, but she is a bit too close to the wall.

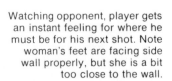

returns by your partner, go back to the fun of predicting where you intend to serve. The fun might turn into embarrassment, but the idea of the drill is to teach you to concentrate on accuracy, thereby improving your control and disproving the notion that racquetball is a random-type game. Your strokes should no longer be random and uncoordinated; they should be purposeful, landing within a six-foot circle of your target. Brumfield told me recently, "On some shots I must hit within two inches of my aiming point or my opponent will have an easy set-up for a kill." No one is asking you to try for two-inch accuracy, but six feet isn't out of the question.

Explanation of center-court positioning

One of the areas of controversy for racquetball pros is center-court positioning. This is a defensive maneuver involving an imaginary circle about six feet in diameter. This circle's outer forward edge starts a foot past the short line in

The transfer of weight from the back of the body to the front seems well organized here, but again, the racquet should be nearly vertical at this position with the handle pointing to the floor. As it's held now the chances are that the ball will go into the ceiling wildly.

center court. This imaginary circle has been called a "defensive headquarters." (A big "X" made of tape, placed four feet back of the short line, can be used as "home base" for center-court position practice.) It is the position to which the racquetball player runs after he or she serves or during a long volley. Mathematically, it's the area that gives the easiest access to all shots returned from the serve. From the center-court position, you have the best chance of racing off in whatever direction your opponent's shot demands.

During the past three years, the ball used in racquetball has become about 20 percent faster. This has, some players feel, moved that invisible circle back somewhat, about four feet back. Faster players have experimented with this with some success.

Drills

Serve and return practice

Now, instead of announcing your serve's target, resolve in your mind where you want to hit and carry out your

When two people practice together, one can hit to the area in which the other needs practice. In this case a forehand stroke to the woman's forehand.

intention. Alternate lobs and drives—left and right, high and low. Try to deceive your opponent. If he or she appears to be playing too close to the short line, use a hard drive to one side or the other. Keep your volleys going. Remember to get back to your center-court position when on defense.

Touch and go

        This is a game that can be played solo, with one player or with two other players. Start the ball moving by hitting it

The touch and go drill is one of the best racquetball practice sequences, because it gets the body moving within a planned framework. The idea is to stand in center court, a few feet behind the short line and hit the ball to the wall. The player then runs to the side wall, touches the wall with her racquet, then races to catch up with the ball if possible. If the student isn't yet advanced enough to keep the ball up and in play, the sequence should be: hit the ball, run to the wall, then run back to center court position. Center court position is a good defensive position, an invisible circle about six feet in diameter that starts a couple of feet back from the short line. After almost every shot, it's a good "headquarters" position for the player to take while waiting for her opponent's next shot. Touch and go, of course, should also include running to the backhand side and touching the backhand side wall.

against the front wall or having your partner serve it to you, preferably slowly, in a lob at first. You then must run to one of the side walls and touch it with your racquet, then pursue and hit the ball. In other words, you must touch the wall with your racquet before you are allowed to hit the ball.

This exercise teaches you that there's usually more set-up time than you think, and it helps you understand that racquetball is a game of motion. One can't and shouldn't stand in one spot and reach out for balls in the neighborhood. The whole court must be your neighborhood, and you should learn to run and play in that neighborhood. Knowing you have a chore to do—touching the wall—before you can hit the ball should force you to use your inherent speed!

Around the world

Line up with your partner (or, if you're practicing in a larger group, with the others) as if at a free-throw line on a

A lob serve to the forehand side.

basketball court. Do this about halfway back between the short line and the back wall. The first person on line lobs the ball to the front wall. The last person on line must run from his or her position "around the world"—that is, around the entire group—and somehow get to the ball and return it. Don't attempt to volley on this one.

Play

By now you should be expert at determining what parts of your game need hard work. Are you lobbing too far from the side walls, giving your opponents easy shots to return? Does your drive serve go into the floor for a skip (floor first) as often as it hits the wall first? Are you not using your backhand? With your areas of weakness in mind, approach the play period constructively, using the shots you're most anxious to improve.

Progress comes quicker in racquetball than in most other sports, and it's possible to have fun in racquetball even if you play poorly and miss many shots, but racquetball is much more fun when you play well, adding a feeling of achievement to the pleasant glow that comes from a good workout.

7

Fifth lesson

1. Brief review of center-court positioning   (2 minutes)
2. Power and quickness development   (8 minutes)
3. Drills
    a. Yarn drill—low
    b. Yarn drill—high
4. Play   (17 minutes)
5. Wrap-up   (3 minutes)

Review

Briefly review center-court positioning, remembering that it is used both for serve and during regular play. Run through a few serves and sprints to center-court position for your return of your opponent's shot.

Power and quickness

In this lesson, we are concentrating on developing accuracy and quickness at the same time. Start the lesson with a drive serve, as low as possible while still falling legally past the short line. Your opponent should try to return the ball as low and as hard as possible. Alternate until you can volley two or three times, low and hard, always remembering to bend from the waist and to hit sideways, either forehand or backhand. The name of this game is to hit below waist level without skipping the ball in. It's not easy. Racquetball has been developing quite swiftly into a power game, and you should begin to utilize some of your own power and learn to defend against your opponent's power.

Drills

Yarn drill

A Chuck Sheftel innovation has been helpful to many beginning racquetballers. Bring a long spool of dark yarn and some tape to the court, and stretch the yarn across the front wall, between two and three feet above the floor.

While standing in the serving area, volley with your partner, trying to hit all your shots below the yarn. You don't have to keep score—just volley with the ball low and legal. Add speed as you gain confidence.

An innovative drill that many of the author's students have found effective is trying to hit the ball under a string or piece of yarn stretched across the court at 18 inches height from the floor. This drill underlines the value of hitting low. The lower you hit the ball the harder it is for your opponent to make a good return against you.

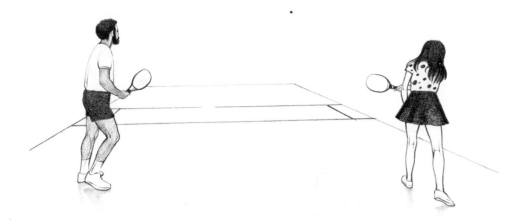

In this drill one person tries to hit the ball back to her own position, then gets out of the way.

Now raise the yarn to a position about six feet high and try playing an entire game with the ball required to hit the front wall below the yarn. You should be able to feel your control growing, and certainly you'll feel yourself "thinking" control in no time at all.

If you survive a first game and aren't too exhausted—as you shouldn't be—lower the yarn two or three feet and play another game.

Play

Remove the yarn but not the mental note to yourself: hit low and hard. Play a regular game in which both you and your partner strive to keep the ball low and hard. Between your good, even great shots and your bloopers, you will soon become aware of what components of your game need work!

Wrap-up

Discuss your strong points and weaknesses with your partner, learning what you can from each other about what you are doing correctly and incorrectly.

8
Sixth lesson

1. Brief review of low placement shots   (2 minutes)
2. Backhand work   (10 minutes)
3. Drills
    a. Feeding backhand   (10 minutes)
    b. Lobs off back wall to backhand   (10 minutes)
    c. Fast drill—all strokes   (10 minutes)
4. Play   (15 minutes)
5. Wrap-up   (3 minutes)

By now you should have a feeling for the kind of warm-up that helps you start your racquetball lesson feeling ready rather than stiff. This hard-earned intelligence about your body and its needs—whether for sit-ups, stretches, or knee bends—should be incorporated into a long-range conditioning plan, possibly involving jogging or swimming, but certainly sit-ups and stretches. Leg raises from a sitting position or while on your back are good. The best conditioned racquetballer on the pro tour, Jay Jones, is a movie stunt man who does yoga every day, but also climbs six flights of stairs ten times!

Brief review of low placement shots

The yarn stretched across the court should have helped you understand that a majority of beginners hit most of their shots too high. Ideally, of course, every shot should be a low kill, but since this is impossible you should keep practicing those low placements, increasing the speed at which you and your partner volley low shots with each other. This improves your coordination and response, as well as your accuracy.

Backhand work

A well-coordinated, smooth backhand is a thing of

Footwork is especially important in this drill. You must be prepared to charge in and hit from that sideways stance.

Server hits to partner's backhand.

beauty and a valuable weapon. Alas, it takes hard work for most people to develop a good backhand. Returning to basics, go over the basic grip and stance from the first two lessons. Practice running to the backhand side and making that slight (quarter-inch) turn of the racquet in your fingers.

Most beginners forget to hold the racquet high enough while running to make a backhand shot. If the racquet is held high enough and far enough back, it saves you last-second raising and positioning.

A good drill is to stay on the left side of the court and imagine that the right side doesn't really exist. The idea, of course, is to use the backhand to the absolute exclusion of your forehand. Your partner should then practice the same way.

Even while practicing alone, you can beef up your backhand by standing on that left side and trying to hit exclusively with your backhand. Kathy Williams, a Detroit pro, finds that her students make excellent progress using a technique called "drop and hit." Just drop the ball with your off hand and backhand it into the wall. Ideally you should be trying to "pinch" the ball into the left wall where it joins the front wall. As long as you can control your backhands sufficiently well to get them into that left-hand corner—by six feet at this stage—you're doing fairly well.

Drills

Feeding backhand

A good two-person drill involves one "feeding" the other's backhand. Crisscross the ball on the court, remembering that the object is to give the backhand a good workout. For some reason—probably degree of difficulty—the poor backhand becomes just that from lack of practice. It is such a marvelous shot, offensively and defensively, that it's worth practicing long and hard.

Lobs off back wall to backhand

Now that you and your partner have achieved a degree of accuracy in your shots, try a series of lobs to the back wall that forces one another to use the backhand off the rear wall. These lobs should hit close to the rear wall; that is, the ball hits the floor, then the rear wall, so that it can be taken on the fly. Don't be afraid to hit a little harder and to vary your feeding habits so that your partner can't tell the target by watching your body. Favor the backhand in this lesson, so that you can learn to depend on it.

Play

In singles, doubles, or cutthroat, use your improving backhand whenever possible, racing to retrieve those leftside shots but also moving your body out of the more natural forehand position into a backhand one. Obviously the name of the backhand game is to keep hitting as many backhands as

Receiver practices taking the backhand off the rear wall.

you can. Depending on how proficient you have become, you will soon be able to control your backhand as well as your forehand.

Wrap-up

With this lesson—its glories and its failures still in your minds—discuss the areas of your game that need practice and plan to improve them.

9

Seventh lesson

1. Briefly review the backhand   (2 minutes)
2. Forehand or backhand?   (8 minutes)
3. Drills
    a. Across and hit   (15 minutes)
    b. Mandatory forehand and backhand   (15 minutes)
4. Play   (15 minutes)
5. Wrap-up   (5 minutes)

You should, of course, still be warming up before entering the court, but now you and your partner should both hit some balls around the court to loosen up. If you're going to play much racquetball, you will probably work out your own regimen of stretches, jogging in place, wall-pushing, and warm-up practice of various shots on court.

Review backhand

A short, brisk review of the backhand in action: favor the backhand stroke as you begin the hour with your partner.

This is the forehand part of forehand-backhand drill, the purpose of which is to give your playing partner practice on both sides of the court.

Try some from deep court, some at mid-court and some up front near the left-hand corner.

Forehand or backhand?

You have been "thinking" backhand. It's now time to return the backhand to perspective—back into your basic game where it will handle about 20 percent of the strokes made during your racquetball career.

The name of this exercise is decisions. You and your partner feed each other balls right through or near center court, and you must decide quickly whether to take them with your backhand or forehand. Your choice will depend in part on the distance you must travel to get back to your defensive headquarters—the center-court position (at the taped "X" four feet back of the short line in mid-court or in that six-foot imaginary circle).

Make your backhand–forehand decision on the basis of the number of steps you'll have to take *after* you make your shot. It's somewhat like instant chess, planning ahead on the court.

Drills

Across and hit

This is a one-person drill, but both of you can do it at the same time, starting from opposite sides of the court.

Stand about six feet back of the short line, along the right-hand wall. Drop the ball and hit it with your forehand so that it returns to you about two steps to the left. You must now hit the ball again, backhand or forehand, to the front wall so that the ball comes back a step or two to your left again. The idea is to work your way across the court. Then, instead of getting angry with yourself for your misses, start back from left to right. Try not to collide with your partner.

You will begin to appreciate what control can do for you with this exercise.

Mandatory forehand and backhand

In this exercise, you start to play. If you receive the

With almost everything working well the player has let the ball arrive a little too close to her body, crowding her swing somewhat. Had she moved several inches straight back, towards the side wall, everything would have been perfect.

serve with your forehand, you must hit your next shot with your backhand, then alternate. This will force you to run and get set for forehands and backhands under game conditions, the kinds you'll run into as you continue in racquetball.

Play

By now you should be able to incorporate backhands and forehands into your game, get into good defensive position, and place the ball fairly close to your target. Your lob serve should cause your opponent some concern along the wall and your drive should be picking up steam as you gain confidence.

You should know when to wait for the ball to come down so that you can powder it, and when to start a mad charge towards the front wall to retrieve a dying near-kill your opponent has executed. In short, you're beginning to play the game.

Wrap-up

Another debriefing session in which you and your partner constructively criticize each other's style of play, shortcomings, and achievements. If there's an empty court available—no charge is made at most clubs for a second hour on an empty court—you might want to work on these criticisms or just play and work out your problems during the game. If you do this, don't get so deeply involved in the game that you can't stop to reenact a good or bad play— always strive to improve.

10

Eighth lesson

1. Review of the past seven lessons   (15 minutes)
2. Drills
   a. Side-wall control test   (5 minutes)
   b. Serve and center play   (10 minutes)
3. A touch of advanced play: Z serves and ceiling
   shots   (10 minutes)
4. Play   (15 minutes)
5. Final wrap-up   (5 minutes)

> Warm up for five minutes.

Review of the past seven lessons

Each partner tries three of each shot: lob serve, drive, backhand return, forehand return, overhand shot, and so on. Stop play each time going down the checklist. Work your way across the court once in the "across and hit" exercise. Take three shots off the back wall with both your forehand and backhand.

Drive serve starts lower than lob serve. Forceful swing is used.

Drills

Side-wall control test

In lesson one, you used the side wall to familiarize yourself with the feel of ball on racquet. Perhaps you were able to hit two or three in a row without a miss. See how many you can do now without missing. It should be a big improvement!

Serve and center play

A taste of future advanced play can be had by continuing to work on your serve for accuracy and speed and to work on your defense by racing back to the center-court position after each serve.

This is a ball control drill. Each player hits his or her own ball and tries to keep going as many shots as possible against the side wall. This drill is alternated with backhands, and finally, in a "pepper" game between the players using one ball.

A touch of advanced play: Z serves and ceiling shots

Try the "Z" serve: stand about five feet from the left wall in the serving area and hit a drive serve that lands on the front wall, about five feet from the right corner. The ball caroms from there down the length of the court and ideally hits the left side wall about five feet from the rear, then heads for the rear wall, completing the letter Z.

This serve, again ideally, sometimes dies in the corner and becomes almost impossible even for pros to return. You can practice it from both sides of the serving area.

The ceiling shot is another advanced maneuver you will encounter in intermediate and advanced play. It is a stroke or even overhand that causes the ball to hit the ceiling within five feet of the front wall and thus bounce way back into the court. The ceiling shot has recently been a fine defensive shot for the pros. It can sometimes give you time to rest and get back into good position from a fall or bad shot. It is generally

Ready-to-hit position could have been improved by having racquet angled towards ceiling, not pointing to back wall. This would leave wrist in better position to "snap" as the ball is hit.

sent down the left wall to your right-handed opponent's backhand.

Men pros are abandoning this shot for power hitting, but some women players have incorporated it into their games. If the ball comes in chest high or lower, you should stroke the ceiling shot sidearm. If the ball is above shoulder height you should hit it overhand, remembering to keep that elbow well back.

Play

Creative shot making is a new trend in racquetball. Be a beginner and use everything you've learned up to this point, but don't be afraid to "create" your own, coordinated shots. That is, sometimes you have to hit when you are off balance or can't get set properly. Don't let the "rules" keep you from trying. You can't do much worse than lose the point!

The backhand part of the forehand-backhand drill. Surprisingly, many new players have better natural backhands than forehands. Some pros feel this is because the necessity of moving the racquet across the body before unleashing it in a stroke gives the arm an easier groove to follow than a forehand that doesn't have the body's support.

Final wrap-up

Well, you've completed the beginner's course that

To achieve good contact with the ball during a late swing. the player is forced into a lurching motion and a slight backwards leaning that will tend to decrease his power. (Observers of Marty Hogan, racquetball's wonder boy, will point out that Hogan often hits from this unbalanced, lurching position. The justification is that Hogan practices four hours a day and does another hour of weight training, permitting him to exert great power from almost any position.)

Chuck Sheftel designed for several thousand successful novices at the six Court Houses in the Chicago area.

Most of those players have gone on to the more advanced courses or have been working on the various aspects of their game as they go along. By now you should have a fine foundation for becoming a good racquetball player.

The secret word is PRACTICE!

Good luck.

Index